Loved to Transparency

By Pat Banks

Copyright Pat Banks

Loved to Transparency

Introduction

In the first book of this three part series entitled *Which Tree*, I addressed some of the issues around the fall of man. I talked about the loss of identity in man and woman. I also talked about what was perhaps the greatest loss of all, the loss of the reality of the goodness of God. It seems as though when man fell he also lost the realization that the One who created him was good, kind, faithful, would not lie and was the only being in all the universe who's motivations were nothing but love. In the fall man and woman lost their transparency with each other and they lost their intimacy with the Father that had been characterized by their daily walks with Him in Garden of Eden in the cool of the day. Even though the Father continued to speak to them, it was not on the same level of the intimate basis that it had been before.

Man had been put out of the garden and was having to work by the toil of his hands and the sweat of his brow; and woman began having great pain in childbirth, and even their relationship changed, her husband was to rule over her. We see throughout Scripture from Genesis until the New Testament came into being, that God's voice became more and more distant, until finally it was totally silent for the four hundred years between the Old and New Testaments.

When Jesus came He came as the light of the world. He came as the voice of God. He came as the lamb that was slain. He came as a full representation of the Father made flesh on the earth: fully man, fully God.

His sacrificial death, burial and resurrection made all things new and available for us that were necessary for us to be able to return to walking in the way we were originally designed - as Adam and Eve originally did in the garden.

2Peter 1:3 *"According as his divine power hath given unto us all things that pertain unto life and godliness, through the knowledge of him that hath called us to glory and virtue*: (KJV)

Chapter 1

In this book we are going to look at the importance of finding our identity as God originally created it. But we're also going to look at the way the enemy has caused us to believe lies about God regarding His goodness, his kindness, about His love and his faithfulness toward us in all situations. We cannot truly live the life that we were created to live without this understanding.

I want you to try to imagine with me for a moment what it would be like to be known at the absolute deepest level of who you are, where you are, known at the deepest, even down to the cellular level of your existence. Further, try to imagine what it would be like to live in a place emotionally, relationally and spiritually, where there is no hiding, no suspicion, no ulterior motive, needing nothing from you; where love and faithfulness is a given.

Imagine being wrapped up in a love that only wants the absolute best for you; and is walking with you trying to help you learn how to walk in that amazing place of absolute freedom and peace. A relationship in which there is no hint of selfish gain, competition, jealousy or lack of any sort, and to be so totally immersed in that love that you are totally and unashamed in any area of your life.

In that place, you're not ashamed of your body, you're not ashamed of your thoughts, you're not ashamed of your feelings, you're not ashamed of your past, you're not ashamed of your present, and you have absolutely no reason to believe that the future could be anything less than amazing.

Then on top of all that, this love and acceptance is made available to you in the context of community relationship. In that community you are connected to another person who equally as loved, equally as transparent, equally without competition, equally without fear, and who only wants to walk with you there and to engage and appreciate everything that has been provided for both of you there.

That is exactly what Adam and Eve had in the Garden of Eden at creation. They had nothing else to compare their lives to. They had no other gauge to know if this was all true or not true. They had nothing other than what they were experiencing to compare their current lives to. They had no other insight, understanding or experience with which to compare their relationship or their surroundings to. Around them was all they could ever want and everything that could possibly be needed. They had it all. And what they had was very good.

I wonder if after a time they became familiar with what they had. I wonder if they grew comfortable in their routine and yet remained excited because they were always learning something new; always experiencing a new level of love and understanding. Always being amazed at the wonder that was found in them and each other, as well as in their surroundings.

Their thinking processes were being developed as they walked in the garden with the Father.

They were learning to embrace all that He said to them by using their minds, in conjunctions with their spirits. They were learning more about each other and how to express themselves. Since God had created them as one, there was complete unity with each other. Since there were no hidden agendas between them, and since fear had never entered the Garden, innocence reigned and consequently, there was no need to figure out how to conduct relationships, how to say things, or resolve relational issues. They were processing all that they were learning together. They were coming to an understanding within themselves of all that was new to them.

Amazingly, one day they were nothing and the next day they had become; and all those maturing and growing processes began. Just as it is with us from the moment of conception, we begin to learn about everything around us. We begin to learn how to communicate. We begin to learn how to process what we are thinking and feeling.

They were also creative beings. We know this because they were created in the Father's image. He is a creative being. He did not control their thoughts. He did not dictate or control the expressions of their creativity. He did not do any of the things that are common to the natural man we know today. He gave them freedom to discover who He was and who they were becoming.

Then, if this is what He wanted for them, and how He wanted them to learn and grow and live, it's easy for us to understand that is what He wants for us. The good news is that because of Jesus, we have access to that life and the power to begin walking as they did.

Chapter 2

Identity... a familiar word, but what is it actually. The dictionary gives several different definitions of identity. We hear identity talked about all the time in the world today. There are dozens of personality tests that are designed to help a person find out who they are and why they act as they do. There are counselors who listen to people every day trying to help them figure out that very same thing and why things aren't working as they should. Never before in the history of the earth have there been more self-help videos, seminars, conferences, podcasts, books, and other materials all designed to try to help people find out who they are. With all those resources available to us one would think that the search to define identity wouldn't take more than a day or two. That raises the question ... do all of these tests, or any of these assessments, actually define our identity for us or is it still just a guess?

They may help us understand our personality, but is that the sum of our identity? I think not.

For the purpose of this book then, this will be the definition of identity as I choose to use it here. The identity of a person is the original design of God as to how that person was created to process life.

Your personality is not your identity, because personalities may change based on life circumstances, age, pain, and other such instances. But the true identity of a person as it relates to my definition suggests that the original design never changes. This means that you and I will always process life through a filter given by God at conception. The way that I express this may change with experience and maturity, but fundamentally it will always be the same lens I see everything through. You and I will certainly grow and mature in many areas and, therefore, we will hopefully express this through increasingly mature and refined responses. However, whether I am happy and excited, sad, angry or silently contemplative, if I am a very black-

and-white, very direct person I will always see things through that lens and my expression of it will fundamentally remain the same.

If I am one who is quiet, and one who doesn't really want to be seen, one who enjoys being alone, I will process life and engage in it through that filter. That filter will be what drives me even though I may be jovial and enjoy being involved with people periodically. Obviously, being such a person I would be comfortable not being seen, because I have no need to be seen. In other words, an eye will always be an eye, a hand will always be a hand and so on.

But before we delve into that further, let's look at Adam and Eve. The Bible says they were created in the image of God. This means they were spirit beings who were also equipped with a body and soul. They were created as three-part beings, much like the Trinity. We know they were physical beings because they were given the responsibility of tending the garden which was a physical garden that required physical activity to tend it and from its production reap the fruit of their labors. Having a brain, they could learn. Having curiosity, or a need to know, along with a voice, they could ask questions. They conversed and interacted with each other. It would seem from Scripture (John 14) that the Father probably communicated with them spirit to spirit.

The Word says He was most easily recognized as a voice walking in the garden with them which would seem to me to indicate that Adam and Eve were indeed spirit beings as well, so that they could hear His spirit voice with their natural ears. (I assume this to be the case because later on in Scripture Moses says, "No man has seen God and lived.")

Because they were pure they were also Transparent – relationally, spiritually, and mentally. The thing that makes something non-transparent is darkness, whether it's caused by woundedness, self-protection, personal sin or something else. If it is totally light, it is transparent. Because the Father is light we know He is transparent. Since they were created in his image they were light as he was light, so they were also transparent. Jesus said He was the light of the world and that we are the light of the world.

Their identity at creation was to simply be those who walk in the light and fellowship with the Father. Those who learn from Him will learn to express themselves to each other, to appropriately relate to the world around them, all the while listening, walking with and learning from the Father. And in this way they would fulfill their purpose for being created. This sounds great doesn't it? If only it were that simple, is the thought most of us have about it. So why is it so hard, even for those who have set their hearts toward living that way? Let's explore some things which make it difficult.

Chapter 3

There are two worlds we must know each other in them. This is an important concept to embrace for without it we are only living a portion of our lives to its fullest advantage. We must know who we are in the spirit, by the Spirit, according to the Word of God. We must know that we are in Him and He is in us, and that we are created in His image and that we are like Him even as He is. And we must know this mutual connectedness through experience with Him, not just head knowledge of a concept. We must learn how the Holy Spirit has defined us and how His Spirit has made us righteous (perfect.) His Holy Spirit has declared to us our identity in Him.

Then there is the natural world which defines our personality and in which we express who we are and why we are here. Our personality determines the way in which we deal with other people in this realm: the way in which we live life. This is the lens through which we begin to understand our purpose and express it.

Yet to merge the spirit world and the natural world is the battle.

Many have determined that they are primarily, if not exclusively, that which relates to the natural world as we know it. It shapes all they see and feel. This belief is compounded by the fact that it is easier to see with our natural eyes and hear with our natural ears. However, according to the Word, we are more spiritual beings than natural beings. In order to begin to properly relate to the spirit realm, we must begin to ask Holy Spirit to open our eyes to the realm of His life. The realm of His eyesight. The things which Jesus talked about when He said let those who have eyes see and those who have ears hear. We must begin to place our faith in that which Holy Spirit says is true, which requires us to learn to hear His voice.

> John 10:27 "*The sheep that are My own hear My voice and listen to Me; I know them, and they follow Me*" (AMP)

We must at some level disconnect from the system of this world that we have been taught as our sole reality.

You will never actually know your true identity until you come into contact and become more and more acquainted with the absolute total never ending faithful compassionate involved love of the Father for you and you alone. But the very thing that caused Man to lose his identity as a transparent totally loved, provided for, cared for, purpose filled child of God is the very thing that still keeps us from walking in that love today.

IS GOD REALLY GOOD? AND GOOD TO ME?

So, all of the personality tests, all of the striving, all of the education, all of the podcasts, all of the books, all of the self-help materials, will not be able to truly restore our own personal identity, that will not happen until we have totally experienced the love of God for ourselves. Realizing that we will never totally be aware of that love in the depth of it, the power of it, the goodness of it until we see Him face-to-face. However, growing in that experiential knowledge, changing in that, maturing in that, and pressing on will bit by bit restore to us to the truth of who we were created to be and who our God really is.

Chapter 4

If you have been a believer very long at all you have heard messages about the issues presented above. Perhaps you have even tried to do things to grab hold of these things. You have studied the Word, fasted and prayed, tried to memorize the Word to renew your mind and many other tactics to come to know truth and walk in it. Yet you still feel like you are stumbling around and not making much progress.

Perhaps the best way to learn how to live this life is to begin in the Garden as was presented in the first book in this series. So now let's begin to unravel some of the issues around living in both worlds; how this distortion has come about as a result of the fall. If we don't understand at some level what is going on, it is hard to come out from under it.

My husband, Jim Banks has written a book entitled "*The Insidious Dance, The Paralysis of Perfectionism*" which deals with our penchant to adopt perfectionism because we are taught and trained in it by the system of this world, the strategy of the enemy himself. It is a great read for more understanding of what is really going on around us and in our belief structures.

At this point we will look at some basic issues that must be addressed if we are to learn how to walk effectively in both worlds.

1. There is a loving trustworthy God who created us and wants an intimate relationship with us.

2. There is an enemy of God who has now become our enemy.

3. The loving God is continually speaking to us and wants us to have abundant life.

4. The enemy is continually speaking to us and wants nothing but death and destruction for us.

5. We are continually speaking to ourselves through self-talk, whether cognitively or not.

6. Whichever voice is the loudest is generally that which sets the direction of our life at any given moment.

The voice of the Lord is truth. The voice of the enemy is a lie. Our voice is somewhere in between. Therefore, the confusion has begun. However, we must learn to hear all three and to easily and quickly distinguish which is which.

The Lord's plan from the beginning was to provide us with value, provision and an enjoyment of Him as His children.

The enemy's plan from the beginning was to derail the Lord's plan. He gave us his tactics as we see him interact with Jesus in the wilderness.

1. Provide for yourself, turn rocks to bread. Use your own strength to live life and get what you need.
2. Try to prove yourself to find value in your life and be accepted by men. Throw yourself off the mountain to prove who you are. Use what you know to protect yourself from harm.

3.   Worship the god of this world, its systems and its ways. Bow down to it.

These are the very things that we deal with today. The old lie that God helps those who help themselves has been fed to many generations, as though His care for us is dependent on our works.

Everything in our culture is setting a standard of what success looks like, or what beauty looks like. In other words, what we have to do to prove we are worth something and that we are of value. Certainly, by achieving those lofty standards eventually we will ARRIVE.

We have bowed down to this system in our thoughts, actions, beliefs, finances, relationships and yes even in our relationship to the Father. "If I do right, everything will be right." I will have ARRIVED.

We are at some level or another either still fighting, or maybe trying to live in denial about these issues. For some they are absolute truth. For others they are recognized for what they are, but are finding it hard to break free from them.

I will occasionally ask people, "If you knew you believed a lie, would you keep believing it?" Most say NO, but the problem is how do I know what truly is a lie and what is truth? And what if after seeing it is as a lie I still choose to believe it because I don't have anything better to replace it with? The reason people have trouble seeing they are believing a lie is rooted in the tree of the knowledge of good and evil.

Chapter 5

The first example, after Adam and Eve, in the scripture of an individual who believed a lie and couldn't see things another way is found in the story of Cain and Abel.

Cain and Abel represent the two trees; one is the spirit of law which is the knowledge of good and evil, the other is the spirit of faith, Spirit of Sonship and trust, which is of the tree of life. The spirit of the law will always try to kill and destroy and get rid of the Spirit of life, that's why in the New Testament Paul says we should,

> *"live by the Spirit of Life in Christ Jesus which has made us free from the law of sin and death."* Romans 8:2 (KJV)

> 5 *"For those who live according to the flesh set their minds on the things of the flesh, but those who live according*

*to the Spirit set their minds on the
things of the Spirit.
6 For to set the mind on the flesh is
death, but to set the mind on the Spirit
is life and peace."* Romans 8:5-6 (KJV)

Cain brought the works of his own hands as
an offering to God who had apparently already
said what was acceptable. In other words,
Cain decided what was good according to his
mind. Abel brought that which was by faith.
Abel brought what God said was good.

The world's system which we live in has been
founded on the tree of the knowledge of good
and evil. We live in a fallen world, with broken
and fallen men who have attempted to
determine what is right and what is wrong.
They have tried to make laws or rules to
ensure that their view of right and wrong are
enforced. And thereby have set a belief system
before us which in most cases is totally
counter to the Tree of life.

Some examples of this might be;

        1. Good men go to heaven, bad men go
to hell.

2. The more a man works and earns money the   more secure he is.

3. Those who achieve the most win in the long run.

4. I have the right to determine my own future.

Or even some religious teachings can be from the wrong tree;

If I'm truly saved I won't sin anymore

I'm saved by grace but my works keep me.

If I don't see it happening it can't be for today.

If I do right everything will be right.

There are many more that need to be examined if we are to break free from the wrong tree. The enemy is subtle and feels very familiar and, in many cases, seems right. All of these familiar patterns have been woven into our thinking and processing systems, thereby distorting the truth. As we have learned these they have become lies we live by. Anything that is contrary to the Law of life in the Spirit is a lie and must be dismantled.

If the preceding thoughts are true, then why is it so hard for us to take the plunge and begin to learn to walk in the Spirit of Life as Christ did when He walked the earth. He said it is possible and also expected of His followers.

There is one big reason; FEAR. It may be fear of man, fear of failure, fear of the unknown, fear of being deceived, fear of loss, fear, fear. The very thing the enemy used to deceive Eve...YOU ARE NOT ENOUGH and GOD Has Deceived you.

Chapter 6

How do we break free of the system of the world and the lies we have believed?

Jesus answered that question fairly directly when He said repent, turn, follow, trust, leave all, and listen. But it would seem easier said than done. So many times, we make up our own truth and a reality that we think fits our belief system better. It is a fact that our belief system and our identity are not only intrinsically entwined, but what we believe determines who we are and what we will respond to, both positively and negatively. This is one of the major reasons why people fight so hard against an opposing opinion. They don't want to change because it might impact who they are.

> "*As a man thinketh in his heart so is he.*"
> Proverbs 23:7 (KJV)

So, there you have it, our belief determines our identity.

The next book will deal with how to find and remove the lies and belief systems that each of us have bought into. It is important to begin to understand how we are wired so that we can then begin to agree with who Jesus says we are and how we can begin to mature in His ways. However, in this book we are going to explore more about what it looks like to walk as spirit beings in a fallen world.

There have many books written and messages preached about this subject and I was very reticent to address it. The Lord however, is never reticent to deal with anything. He said keep it simple with the understanding you have, and I will bring some revelation to those who read it, if they want it. He also said that He taught in simple ways so I should rely on Holy Spirit to do the revealing. So here goes from my simplistic perspective.

Jesus walked in the seen world and in the unseen (spirit realm) world at the same time.

He said, "*I only do what I see my Father doing.*"

Does that mean He looked around on earth to see what was happening? I think not. That is why He taught His disciples to pray, *"Thy Kingdom come on earth as it is in heaven."* He saw what was in heaven and released it on earth. The word says in 1John4:17,

> *"In this way, love has been perfected among us, so that we may have confidence on the day of judgment; for in this world we are just like Him."* BSB

Would this then not establish that if He did it, we can do it as well? If He saw, we can see. If He heard we can hear. If He knew His identity and purpose, so can we! Notice that it doesn't say in the sweet by and by. It says WE ARE JUST LIKE HIM....now.

Well, that definitely seems like a far-fetched idea to me when I look at the experiences of my own life. But that is exactly what it says in every translation, I checked.

In John 14:20 Jesus says,

> *"When I am raised to life again, you will know that I am in my Father, and you are in me, and I am in you."*

So again, if He did it, and said it, so can we.

Let's look at the life of Jesus and see if that helps us learn how to live like He lived.

His purpose and destiny were breathed into Him in His mother's womb. Mary knew from the get-go even though she may not have understood it all. (Of course, it didn't hurt to have an angel announce it to her.) So, we might think, well there you have it, Jesus got a head start on us. But the scripture says in Jeremiah 1:5 NAS,

"I knew you before I formed you in your mother's womb."

So, in this verse there is another precedent for identity and purpose coming from the Father. Unless you believe the Father has a few favorites and the rest of us are after thoughts with no purpose or plan from the Father, then Jesus did not have a head-start on us.

The first recorded account of Jesus himself talking about purpose and destiny was when the family went to Jerusalem and He stayed behind.

> *"And Jesus increased in wisdom and stature, and in favor with God and man."* Luke 2:52 KJV

This was recorded after Jesus was in the Temple teaching in Jerusalem and His parents didn't know where He was. At that time, He was 12 years old. He said He had to be about His father's business. I wonder if they thought He meant because He was a Jew, and He was being about Abraham's business. Hmm ... just a thought.

What I want us to look at though is how He grew. It says He grew in Wisdom.

> *"The fear of the LORD is the beginning of wisdom: and the knowledge of the Holy One is understanding"*. Proverbs 9:10 (NAS)

It's interesting how many times Wisdom, understanding and knowledge are linked together in scripture. The above verse would say that He feared the Lord and sought knowledge about Him, and in that process, He gained understanding. So, He came to know the ways of the Father through fear of the Lord, asking for wisdom and then gained understanding about what He was being taught.

I believe He knew to ask for wisdom because of James 1:5 NAS

> "*But if any of you lacks wisdom, let him ask of God, who gives to all generously and without reproach and it will be given to him.*"

Because Jesus was fully human He had to learn, even as we do. So, the first steps to learning how to live as He did, after becoming His children should be to gain a Fear of the Lord, ask for Wisdom and let it bring Understanding. To do these things requires focus, humility and discernment in hearing. Focus on who the God we are related to really is. Then in a posture of humility, ask for His wisdom, and the spiritual discernment for understanding of what we were given actually means. Interesting to note that the verse in Proverbs: 9:10 says that, "*knowledge of the Holy One is understanding.*" So true wisdom should teach us about the Father and His ways.

Why do I say humility is needed to ask for Wisdom? It goes back to the Tree of the Knowledge of Good and Evil. Proverbs 21:2 (NAS)

> "*Every man's way is right in his own eyes, But the LORD weighs the hearts.*"

Remember eating from the wrong tree is basically determining what is right and wrong based on our own knowledge ... and your own terms.

Jesus had twelve years of learning and understanding the things of God before we ever hear of Him. It was not an instantaneous event, it was a process. He stayed in the process and so must we. In our day and time, we want everything now, but to learn the Fear of the Lord and Understanding of the Holy one takes a lifetime of humility and you must become a life-long learner. The question is then how much do you want it?

Proverbs 9:10 states,

> "*The starting point for acquiring wisdom is to be consumed with awe as you worship Jehovah-God. To receive the revelation of the Holy One, you*

must come to the one who has living-understanding." (TPT)

Chapter 7

The last few chapters have given us an idea of how Jesus came to walk as He did, and we can see where we should begin. So now let's look at some of the evidences of how He walked and how it looked. This is where the choice to believe or not believe that we are in the world as HE is and was and forever will be in the world, will be made manifest.

The next main event that gives us a picture of how Jesus walked into His purpose and destiny is at His Baptism which recorded in Matthew 3:13-17;

> *13 "Then Jesus arrived from Galilee at the Jordan coming to John, to be baptized by him. 14 But John tried to prevent Him, saying, "I have need to be baptized by You, and do You come to me?" 15 But Jesus answering said to*

him, "Permit it at this time; for in this way it is fitting for us to fulfill all righteousness." Then he permitted Him. 16 After being baptized, Jesus came up immediately from the water; and behold, the heavens were opened, and he saw the Spirit of God descending as a dove and lighting on Him, 17 and behold, a voice out of the heavens said, "This is My beloved Son, in whom I am well-pleased."

Jesus understood He had to walk in obedience to the Law that was in place at that time in order to fulfill His purpose. He humbled himself and that required John to Baptize Him. The Father then anointed and sealed Him with the Holy Spirit. And followed it up with a declaration of Jesus' identity and His pleasure with Him.

What that says to us is we have to be faithful where we are to do what's right until God's time for us. Then we must humble ourselves before others, usually those in charge. We then must receive the anointing of the Father and His blessing. Now this does not mean a one-time thing that everything in our lives leads up to. This happens as soon as we start entering into the process talked about above. You may say well I have been baptized already, or I have received the Holy Spirit already.

So then have you heard His pronouncement that you are His child and He is well pleased with you? Look at the order and you will see it is necessary in our daily lives. Walk in obedience, walk in humility and daily die to yourself and live to Him. We can be assured that His Spirit will bear witness with us and anoint us for that which is to come.

But hold your horses!!!! Look what comes next. Yes, you know the story, but look how it relates to us again. The wilderness was part of God's plan to prove Jesus was fulfilling His purpose by His own choice. The Enemy tested Him in three areas as we said before. He tested Him with providing for Himself, tested Him with approval and the adulation of men, and tested Him with power.

These are the main issues we have to deal with on a daily basis and I believe the Father is showing us that we can overcome them and not bow down to our own carnal thinking. We can trust that when we have walked in obedience, humility and knowledge of who our God is, He will show us when we are being tempted in one of these areas, so we can overcome it.

The result will be so effective that the enemy will have no place in us, just as He had none in Jesus. This is not a salvation issue, it is a becoming like Him in our soul man issue. It is working out the power and the benefit of our salvation. Jesus actually performed miracles in these very areas He was tempted with. He multiplied bread to feed the hungry, out loud and before men He asked the Father to prove who He was by performing what Jesus was asking, and instead of throwing himself off a pinnacle, He hung himself on a cross. Sometimes our greatest temptations can become our greatest miracles.

Chapter 8

Now, on to the next part of learning how to begin the process of walking as Jesus walked.

When Jesus came out of the wilderness after forty days of fasting, He found those He was to walk with during the next portion of His life. In doing so He showed the importance of relationships. Sometimes it seems that the disciples are portrayed as projects for Him to fix. However, Jesus called them friends. Yes, He showed them how to live and helped them through their stuff, but His primary purpose was to show them how to love and give them their purpose. Then He would give them an opportunity to obey, humble themselves and believe who their God really was.

Notice that after His death they went into a wilderness of sorts and had to wait for the anointing of Father to come on them. It was harder for some of them to believe who He said they were than others. But the ones who believed went on to change the world.

Something else worth noting is that when Jesus called them, He told them what they were going to do before they knew who they were. He knew it all along. He knows who you are and is currently working in your life to help you finally believe and become who you are; along with knowing your specific purpose and your unique identity.

As He walked with people it became evident by how he conducted His life who He was. It should be the same with us. It wasn't the miracles that changed them it was His life. The miracles were just points of emphasis. Peter said, '*Lord you have the words of eternal life*'. His daily conversation brought them into life. Our daily lives are more important to our identity than the miracles or works we might do.

Chapter 9

Now let's transition to how do we learn to walk in the Spirit. What does life in the Spirit actually look like? What does it mean to walk in the spirit?

The transition we need to make is to think that what it means is that we see things that aren't as though they are. This is the ultimate goal of renewing our minds. We will begin to see possibilities rather than problems. We will begin to see the plan of God rather a dim view of the way things have always been. It means we will see creatively rather than replicated another version of what someone else has already done. It means that we see God's design in everything.

It means that we will see beyond what our natural eyes are limited to seeing and we will see with our God given imagination. We will be stirred by God, and like Him, we will creatively speak things into existence. It means that we will see and speak things that aren't as though they already are. That actually sounds like faith to me.

Jesus had the ability to discern. He learned by having his senses trained. His senses were trained to turn toward the Father. The Word says that we should have our senses trained to discern between good and evil. What is that really? Basically, this training is learning to discern whether something comes from the tree of the knowledge of good and evil, or the tree of life.

The Word says that we are to work out our own salvation. This doesn't mean that we are to work for our salvation, or that we are to figure it out. Neither does it mean that we have to try our hardest to obey so that we can be good enough to receive a reward on Judgment Day. I believe it is saying that we need to learn. We need to work and study. We need to become trained. But most of all we need to ask Holy Spirit, who indwells us, to show us which tree we are eating from.

However, doing those things without involving ourselves in becoming the spiritual beings that we were created to be, could cause us to simply take what we have learned and filter it through the wrong tree. We need to be training ourselves to discern if are listening to the tree of the knowledge of good and evil, or listening and learning from the tree of life. We need to begin to train ourselves. We need to be conscious of it.

We need to spend time in the spirit realm and in the presence of the Father; spending time in the presence of Jesus. We need to be learning from their presence and absorbing the marvel of who they are. While drawing in close to them we can begin to examine the things that Jesus did, from a spiritual perspective, not that of our natural minds.

Jesus was always aware of the Spirit realm. He knew every detail, even when people were doubting. He knew when they were coming to kill Him. He knew when and where angels were available to Him. He knew the voice of His Father was not found just in the scrolls. He knew His voice had creative power. He used it when He multiplied the bread. He used it to calm the waters. He used it to heal people.

Our voices also have power to create in the Spirit realm. How do I know this? Because He says we are like Him! Our words have tremendous creative power. The Word says life and death are in the power of the tongue. I don't believe life and death are strictly our bodies checking in or checking out.

Again, I believe it has everything to do with which Tree we are feeding on and releasing. Jesus only released life.

> 1. Am I willing to believe that my purpose and destiny were breathed into me while I was in my mother's womb?

> 2. Am I willing to set our hearts toward asking for wisdom walking in humility and coming to understand the Holy One?

> 3. Am I willing to stay in the process?

> 4. Am I willing to move when he says move?

> 5. And conversely, Am I willing to stop when He says to stop?

6. Am I willing to walk in obedience, walk in humility and wait for the manifestation of anointing upon me?

7. Am I willing to go through the wilderness knowing that He is with me, perfecting me and preparing me?

8. Am I willing to walk in community giving life to others and receiving life from others?

9. Am I willing to believe that I am more than just a natural being and begin to have my senses trained to discern the things of the spirit?

If all these things are true, and you want them, then it is time to intentionally schedule time in the presence of God, time in the Word, time in community, time in training, time in hope, time in faith. It is time to eat from the tree of life and only speak life. It is time to create. It is time to create hope, time to create joy, time to create life as Jesus did when he walked on the earth because He said, 'As He is so are we in the earth.'

Does all of this sound like work and hard? Well, He didn't say it would be easy, but ask yourself this question? Is what I am doing now changing me into the person I was created to be? Is it letting love rend veils around my heart and mind to more fully comprehend His love for me and the world? Is my determined purpose to know Him?

> *"And this is life eternal, that they should know thee the only true God, and him whom thou didst send, eve Jesus Christ....." John 17:3 (NAS)*

This is our purpose. This is our identity. This is LIFE.

About the Author

Pat Banks, the youngest of four children, was born and raised in Kansas. Her father got saved later in life, while she was in Grade School, and within a couple of years surrendered to go into full-time ministry. She graduated High School in Sharon Springs, KS and shortly thereafter moved to Fort Worth, TX to take on the world. Following a move to Houston, she enrolled in college and began working for Southwestern Bell Telephone. It wasn't long before she became an executive trainer for the company.

In late 1979 she met Jim Banks and they were married the following year, moving immediately to Indianapolis, Indiana where she resumed her career with Southwestern Bell. From that point until they entered ministry full time, they ministered on nights and weekends, leading small groups, discipling and teaching Bible studies. After raising four children and following a move from the Atlanta area to Asheville, NC in 2002 they decided to leave the corporate world for good. Ministry has been their sole focus ever since.

Pat is still "a trainer," a teacher, a public speaker, an inner healing and deliverance minister, and now an author, dedicated to loving God and loving people.

Which Tree?

Patricia Banks

72 pages

ISBN-13: 978-1537304649
ISBN-10: 153730464X

This book is first in a series of three covering the Two Trees in the Garden of Eden and how to reclaim the individual identity which was lost as a result of the fall of man. This series will deal with how to live as the spiritual beings we were originally designed to be. There is a decided difference in the effects of which tree you live from today. One will bring life in the Kingdom of God, the other only brings the semblance of life offered by the world.